29569576R00073

Printed in Great Britain
by Amazon